On Revolution

meditations

Ya'Ke Smith

BookLeaf Publishing

India | USA | UK

Made with ❤ on the BookLeaf Publishing Platform

www.bookleafpub.in

www.bookleafpub.com

Dedication

for my son
and all children
I hope we don't fail you
I hope we fight hard to create a better world for you to
live in

Preface

When we look around the world, we are confronted by borders: psychological borders, physical borders, sexual borders, spiritual borders, racial borders. These borders are meant to control us, to restrict us to remain within the confines of what the powers that be deem as healthy — what *they* perceive to be normal. These borders are meant to confine us. To keep us in line. To box us in so tightly that the only thing we can think about is our survival. When one's energy is all expended towards surviving, they have no strength to fight back against the system that put them in that position in the first place. This is a very deliberate tactic.

As a social justice artist, filmmaker, gatherer of words, and professor who urges his students to think of the social and political implications of the work they create, I believe that as long as there are walls, borders and mechanisms of confinement, that there must be movements of liberation that resist those systems. We, the American people, can no longer wait for change — we must demand it, and more than that, we must take it by force.

The rich. The poor. The privileged. The disadvantaged. Every race. Every gender. CEO's. Food service workers. Janitors. K-12 teachers. University professors and administrators. (Fill in your occupation). We are all under attack, and we are all collectively responsible for dismantling this current oligarchical regime.

This book doesn't just consist of words, it is composed of revolutionary weapons. It is my noise maker, my clarion call, me screaming into the universe, hoping it hears, praying it responds, but knowing that if it doesn't, that I must still demand change by any means necessary. It's my plea to the citizens of earth to not bow down to the tyrannical government that is trying to destroy us. I hope something written within these pages inspires you. Challenges you. Provokes you. Heals you.

My prayer is that when you put this book down that you are baptized in the spirit of revolution and are ready to take action.

Our survival depends on it.

Acknowledgements

those who have died in the pursuit of freedom.
those who are continuing the fight.
those who are slowly waking up to the revolutionary
that exists within them.

on america

To say that I don't recognize this place would be a lie.

I've seen her before.
In the bellies of slave ships.
On burned out buses.
In small pox infected blankets.
In internment camps.
In deadly experiments conducted
on her own people.

I've seen her in redlining.
Heard her in the music of chain gangs.
Smelled her as the smoke of charred
bodies filled the night sky.
Watched her tears create oceans of lies
that turned into blood.
Witnessed her commit genocide in the
name of God — In the name of God
I've observed her bring confusion and despair.

I've seen her bury school children in
unmarked graves.
Witnessed her jail innocent people
who dared challenge her assault on them.

I've felt her in the currents of rivers,
as tortured and dismembered
bodies were exhumed.

I've heard her proclaim the name of Jehovah,
as she slit throats and broke necks.

I wish I could say I don't recognize this place.

Hadn't heard this voice.

Hadn't smelled this pungent scent in my nostrils.

But that would be a lie.

She's been here all along.

Lying in wait from the beginning.

on dissent

We go along to get along.

We go along to acquire riches and fame.

We go along to be in the room
with the *it* person
in the *it* moment.

We go along for likes and shares
and affirming comments from
people we do not know.

We go along for the chance to speak on stages
with lights that illuminate us so brightly that we
no longer recognize ourselves.

We go along for so long that we can no longer decipher
the sound of our voice — no longer recognize the
heart that beats within us.

We go along so long that we can no longer see them for
what they are, because we've become them.

We've become the *them* that picks the people apart limb
by limb.

Because we didn't dissent, we've become tyrants.

on reincarnation

If you shoot me
my blood will splatter throughout the earth
and
find
hosts
to live inside of
and duplicate itself.

If you burn me
the wind will carry my ashes
to the lungs
of those waiting to
breathe
in
deeply
my
spirit
of
revolution.

If you stone me, the rocks will cry out in search of
hands
to
build
temples of worship
where
songs
of
praise
will
be
sung.

If you bury me alive, my roots will burrow so deep into
the earth that the one who persecuted me
will
be
forced
to
eat
the
sustenance
from
my
trees.

You see, this flesh you kill is only one part of me.
It's
the
least
powerful
component
of
who
I
am.

on memory

Books bans are not about paper and ink,
but the erasure of memory.

Remembering is traumatic because it forces
the autocratic into a deep state of rememory,
a state where the fairy tales they concoct can
no longer exist, because the spirit of those buried
by their lies is exhumed.

The smell of burned flesh permeates their nostrils.

The sound of feet cut off as they made their way
towards freedom shake the foundation of their homes.

The trembling voices that sang in agony force them
to reckon with their deceptions.
It foils their ability to hide behind the warped history
that has protected their bloodline.

The words buried in the pages of books possess the
power to stop tyranny, because tyranny is fueled by lies,
deceit and misinformation.

To toss the book into the fire is to throw away the
roadmap of escape, because it makes those that escaped
the enemies of freedom.

It allows for the oppressor to appear oppressed.

Their history goes something like this:
Remember Jefferson,
but not Hemmings.

Remember the White House,
but not the bloody hands that built it.

Wrap yourself in comfortable bed sheets,
but forget the millions of Black bodies that
made cotton a global goldmine.

We imprison criminals,
not innocents whose shackled bodies
make us wealthier by the day.

Text until your fingers bleed,
but don't think of the countless men, women and
children who have been buried under the rubble of
cobalt mines.

The books that they want to remain give cover to the
purveyors of violence.

They cut out the tongues of those that died at their
hands.

Words are an evocation of memory,
but their words,
and their memory
is a delusion.

on revolutionary children

Do not cut out their tongues,
let them chant.

Do not strangle their necks,
let them breathe out in radical revolution.

Do not cut off their feet,
let the reverberations of their march
their stomp
their dance
topple the empire that attempts to paralyze them.

Do not leave them unshielded,
open and vulnerable to the attacks of those who
would see them silenced by any means.

Let the children do the work of bringing down systems
of oppression.

Let the children do the work that our comforts
and responsibilities
and fears
stop us from doing.

Free the children to do the work of liberating us all.

12

on prayer

Praying is about searching.
Searching for answers.
Searching for roadmaps to private and public liberation.

Prayer is about connection.
Connection to something bigger than yourself.
Connection to a source that gives solace to your soul
and to the souls that live in the world around you.

Prayer reveals truth — connects you to *the* truth.

Prayer is about surrendering to the quiet whispers of
God.

Prayer is about submitting
not to own your whims,
but to the whims of the wind,
letting it blow you where you are destined to go.

Prayer is not passive,
it empowers one to take action against their enemies.

Fervent and unwavering prayer brings down the walls of
oppression, because it marries your spirit with that of
the great liberator.

Prayer exorcises the satanic and maniacal forces that
mount themselves against you.

Prayer is the exhalation preserving you and those closest
to you.

Prayer is the most revolutionary act there is, because the
breath of your prayer keeps the rebellion alive.

on fear

I feel the debilitating weight of uncertainty.
A weight so heavy that it kills me
then brings me back to life
so it can watch me die over and over again.

This weight doesn't want to destroy me permanently
but relishes in the anxiety I feel from the anticipation of
my undoing.

The point of this terror is fear.
Fear that would leave me too paralyzed to fight back.
Too debilitated to cry out for help.
Too emotionally wrecked to be anything other than
broken.

But fear and terror have never stopped a revolution.
They have never been able to disrupt the radical
advancement towards liberation.

Fear didn't stop Lumumba.

Fear didn't stop Guevara.

Fear didn't stop X

or King

or Hamer

or Chisholm

or Gandhi

or Mandela

or Davis

or Huerta

or Chavez

or Newton.

Fear didn't halt Nat Turner's Rebellion

or the Haitian Revolution

or Gaspar Yanga's Rebellion

or Pontiac's Rebellion

or the Suffrage Movement

or the American Indian Movement

or the Civil Rights Movement.

Fearing me into silence and paralysis is the goal, because empire knows that fear thwarts freedom.

on artists

When they come for the artists
they come to create the narrative
that they fabricated the truth.

They come to obliterate the images
of those that lived through their barbarism,
their ethnic cleansing,
their murderous traditions of oppression.

When they come for the artists
they come to erase the archives,
the narratives of tyranny and suffering
that they forced the people to endure.

They come to change the language
terrorists: not children
thugs: not teenage boys and girls
criminals: not political hostages
animals: not human beings
Because to kill a terrorist, a thug, a criminal is
(in their mind) a God given duty.

When they come for the artists
they come to stifle the people's will,
to shackle the liberated,
to destroy the resistance that can dismantle their
oppressive powers.

When they come for the artists, they come for the truth.

on silence

Silence isn't golden, it's rotten to the core.
It may bring opportunities, but it will not bring peace.

Turn the other cheek, they say.
Forgive your neighbors, they say.
But in these perilous times
turning and forgiving
means someone dies with your blessing.

Silence brings temporary comfort,
maybe riches and fame,
but after you've adorned yourself
with silence's gold and silver,
fattened yourself with its milk and honey,
an indescribable emptiness will consume you.
You know deep down that your silence
is aiding in the demise of our species.

Silence will haunt you,
bringing the terror that you thought it would protect
you from right to your bedside,
bumping in the night,
filling your heart with angst and regret.
The debilitating pain of the ones who died
because the enemy of the people had your tongue too
tied to utter a word in their defense will haunt you.

Silence will not stop wars
will not cease violence
will not end suffering.
It is the root cause of all suffering.

Silence isn't silence at all.
It speaks louder than any voice ever could.

on christian nationalism

What would Jesus do?

Would he go to church?

If so, where?

Would he sing in the choir?

Would he rob the poor in his name,
declare the native people of a region as witches needing
to be exorcised of their demonic beliefs?

Would he sit amongst those that bomb children in one
breath and decry abortion in the next?

Would he ride on tanks that trample villages in order to
steal
their land,
their money,
their bodies for free labor?

Would he protect the right to bear arms while looking
away from the blood of innocent people
smeared on school desks,

grocery store coolers,
church pews,
sajjadahs,
kippahs,
hijabs?

Would he aid in the destruction of an entire race of
people for financial gain?

Would he preach hate in his father's name?

Would this Palestinian refugee close the border to those
searching for a safe place where they can pick up the
broken pieces of their lives?

Would he accept manifest destiny or the doctrine of
discovery as God's law?

Would he pull up to a rally and attempt to, in the name
of God, run down everyone in his path?

Would be preach about money while his children are
starving?

Would he lead with anger?

Would he move through the world in fancy clothes and cars and accessories while most of humanity can barely afford to provide their families with basic needs?

What exactly would Jesus do?

on solidarity

Divide and conquer.
Chaos and control.
This is the enemy's tool of occupation.

It's not his might
nor his power
nor his strength
that renders us helpless.
It's his ability to turn brother against brother
father against son
mother against daughter
oppressed person against oppressed person
that allows him to topple us.

He knows that a common song
a unified march
a harmonious cacophony of music and words
brought down the walls of Jericho.

He knows that a common tongue
a common kingdom to overthrow
a common corrupt system to be dismantled
a common strategy to bring justice and equity
is how we win this war of attrition.

Holding hands is not only for the lovestruck
it is for the war torn
for the disqualified
for the downtrodden
for the children of suffering and suffocation.

Breathing the same breath.
Feeling the same hope.
Fighting on one accord.
That's how we defeat *our* enemy.

on faith

It's difficult to believe you can swim when you're
drowning.

To see fifty-feet ahead of you when the fog is so dense
it's blinding.

It's almost impossible to remain calm when war has
broken open the deepest
part of your being — stolen all you held dear.

It's painful to dance when there is no music.
Paint where there is no canvas.
Move when your feet have been cut off at the ankles.

But faith requires blindness in order for it to work.

It requires seeing light in darkness.

It requires smiling through tears.

It requires seeing visions of freedom while in bondage.

It requires tasting the fruit of abundance while in famine.

It requires the persecuted to fight through what they can see, and create the world they know they deserve to live in —to envision the future world they want their children to inhabit.

Unwavering faith is the only way to true liberation.

on love

When asked what the most important commandment
was, Jesus answered: *Love your neighbor as yourself.*

But what does it mean to love someone you may not
understand with the same love that you offer to yourself.
To see them as flesh of your flesh and bone of your bone.
To welcome them in to breathe the same air that you
breathe.

It begs the questions:

would I bomb myself?

starve myself?

destroy the animals that bring me sustenance?

poison the rivers that irrigate my land
that cleanse my body
that keep me alive?

would I shoot my own children?

could I stand and watch them killed by a person who
deems their existence as dispensable?

can I love my neighbor in spite of our differences —in
spite of the gulf between us?

How can I profess love if I don't see your face in mine.

on self care (while fighting the revolution)

Take care of yourself.

Protect your mind.

Find peace within.

Baptize your spirit with the waters
of joy
and family
and laughter
and kisses
and love.

Find time to fuck
and dance
and sing
and pray
and be still.

You deserve euphoria.

You deserve communion with yourself.

You deserve unbridled connection with God.

You deserve silence and stillness.

You deserve a break from consuming it all.

Fighting while exhausted is political suicide,
and this self-sabotage is what your enemy is banking on,
because they know that self care,
leads to care for the community,
which is a key component of revolution.

on nature (and its warnings)

Fires raging.

The only thing left to breathe in is toxic ash
destroying us from the inside out.

Planes falling out of the sky
even the air is strangled from this new wind.

Like Jonah, whales are swallowing men whole,
and then giving them back to the water whole
because of repulsion with the human soul.

Epidemics and pandemics on rotation
countless lives taken way too soon.

Creatures from the abyss are being vomited up,
bringing even more unknown parasites into plain sight.

Water is causing disease.

Food is causing disease.

Diseases are reproducing with each other
giving birth to new disease.

Tears of hopelessness water the grass.

The wind sings a warning song, one that if we don't heed, will morph into a dirge.

on subversives

Grin.

Bear it.

Don't let them see you sweat.
Don't let them know what you're thinking.

Grin.

Bear it.

Don't let them know you're hurting.
Don't let them watch you bleed from the knife
they thrusted into your back.
Go heal in the darkness of night,
away from their murderous eyes.

Go convalesce in the arms of those that were
wounded before you.
Be healed by their hands.
Resurrected by their songs.
Revolutionized by their secret whispers.
Radicalized by their detailed plans of escape.

Listen closely as they instruct you:
Commune with your ancestors.

Don't forget to Smile.

*Create your map to freedom in the form of an intricately
stitched quilt.*

Keep smiling.

*Sing your war cry in the harmonious and beautiful key
of a spiritual.*

Grin.

I know they're trying to kill you.

Bear it for just a bit longer.

I know you're tired of warding off your enemies.

Smirk for a moment more.

Don't let them see you coming.
Draw them in closer with your soft eyes.
Reject their assault.
Deny them your dollar.

Remove them from your presence.
Fight them on your own terms.
Disarm them with your smile,
and without them knowing
storm their camp and take back what's yours.

on temples

I wonder if God would exist without a palace.
Without a temple built to utter the names of God.
Without a shrine to feel God's presence.

I wonder if God would exist if we didn't gather
in the thousands.
If only two or three of us gathered together in
the name of God
to profess God's being
to profess God's goodness
to worship God in spirit and truth.

I wonder if God would exist if the altars we built
weren't etched in silver and gold,
if they weren't made of marble or alabaster
so pristine that the light reflecting off of them blinds us.

I wonder what would happen if we actually asked God
where God wanted to exist.

God would say:
In the mouths of my children.
In the hearts of humanity.
In the mind.

In kindness.
In meekness.
In mercy.
In love.
In patience.
In a sweet embrace.
In bodily temples of the Holy Spirit.

on prophets

Every generation deserves a prophet.
One who has the ear of the world.
One who uses their voice to shake
us awake and disrupt our comforts.
One who places a mirror in front of
us so we can see our reflection.

Every generation needs an oracle.
One with the boldness to say the things
that many of us are afraid to say.
One who would rather face death than
stay silent, because for them — silence is death.

Every generation needs a visionary.
One who speaks truths that not only
hold weight during their lifetime,
but that also reverberate into a future
they will never inhabit.
One whose words warn us of trouble to come,
and if we listen closely, give us the tools
to wage war on our oppressors.

Every generation needs a Godly seer.
One filled with the spirit of revolt.
One who isn't afraid to disrupt the status quo.
One who doesn't cower.
One who isn't afraid to challenge anything that
stands in the way of progress.
One who bears witness, even if what they see
shatters them into a thousand pieces.

Every generation needs a spirit filled mouthpiece.
One who understands that their life is not their own.
One who heeds the call from God to speak truth to
power even though the powerful threaten to disappear
them.

Every generation deserves a prophet.

One who can foresee a future paradise in this current
hell.

One who knows that a new world is gestating in the
womb of time, waiting for revolutionary midwives to
bring her into being.